SEA TURTLES

A TRUE BOOK

by

Emilie U. Lepthien

Children's Press®
A Division of Grolier Publishing

New York London Hong Kong Sydney
Danbury, Connecticut

Reading Consultant
Linda Cornwell
Learning Resource Consultant
Indiana Department of
Education

A green sea turtle

Library of Congress Cataloging-in-Publication Data

Lepthien, Emilie U. 1946–
    Sea Turtles / by Emilie U. Lepthien.
        p.   cm. — (A true book)
    Includes bibliographical references (p.   ) and index.
    Summary: An introduction to sea turtles: where they live, what they
eat, how they breed and nest, and more.
    ISBN 0-516-20161-1 (lib. bdg.)   ISBN 0-516-26113-4 (pbk.)
    1. Sea turtles—Juvenile literature. [1. Sea turtles. 2. Turtles.] I. Title.
II. Series.
QL666.C536L46 1996
597.92—dc20   96-13925
                                                                    CIP
                                                                    AC

Contents

This diorama shows how the earth may have looked during the time of dinosaurs (top). A fossil of an ancient turtle (bottom)

At Home In the Sea

Turtles have been around for a very long time. Scientists have found evidence that turtles lived during the era of the dinosaurs—more than 185 million years ago.

At that time, reptiles, including dinosaurs and turtles, dominated the earth.

Sea turtles spend most of their time in the ocean.

But over thousands of years,
the earth's climate changed.
In order to survive, turtles had
to change too.

One type of turtle gradually
made its home in the ocean.
Females came ashore only to
lay their eggs. By adapting to
their new environment, sea
turtles continued to thrive. In
recent times, however,
people have brought them
close to extinction.

Today, there are many different kinds of turtles. These include mud turtles, musk turtles, soft-shelled turtles, tortoises, and sea turtles.

Like all turtles, sea turtles have shells. Turtles are the

Sea turtles, like all turtles, have shells.

only reptiles that have protec-
tive bony shells around their
bodies. The upper shell is
called the *carapace*. It is
joined to a bottom shell
called the *plastron*. Each shell

9

has two layers. The inner layer is made of tightly joined bones. The outer layer is a thin, horn-like material made of scales called *scutes.*

Like all turtles, sea turtles breathe oxygen and have a long life span. All turtles are cold-blooded. This means that their body stays at about the same temperature as the air or water around them.

A sea turtle's shell is less rigid than that of a land-

A sea turtle's body is softer and more streamlined than the body of a land turtle.

dwelling turtle, and its carapace is flatter. A sea turtle's
body is more streamlined.
This helps it swim.

A land turtle (left) can withdraw completely into its shell. A sea turtle (above) can pull back only slightly into its shell.

The shells of other turtles are dome-shaped for protection. Box turtles, for example, can retreat completely into their shells. When they feel threatened, they pull their head and legs inside their shell and snap it shut.

Sea turtles, however, can pull their heads back only slightly into their shells. They have fewer bones in their shells, which makes them lighter in the water.

Male sea turtles spend their entire lives in the sea. Females come ashore only to lay their eggs. All sea turtle species are endangered.

Sea Turtle Species

There are seven types of sea turtles: flatback, green, loggerhead, leatherback, Kemp's ridley, Pacific ridley, and hawksbill.

Most types of sea turtles are found in the warm waters of the world. The Gulf Stream carries them to Europe and Africa. Several species nest along the coasts of Florida

A loggerhead sea turtle (above) and a hawksbill sea turtle (right)

and as far west as Texas. Others find good nesting sites along the coasts of Mexico and Central and South America.

Flatback sea turtles live off the coast of Queensland, Australia, and in the Torres Straits. They also nest along the 1,200-mile (1,920-kilometer) Great Barrier Reef.

Leatherbacks are the largest sea turtles. In fact, they are the largest of all living turtles. They weigh 1,000 to 1,300 pounds (450 to 585 kilograms). The carapace of a leatherback may be a whopping 9 feet (2.7 meters) long!

Ridleys are the smallest sea turtles. Most adult ridleys weigh

A leatherback sea turtle (above) and a Kemp's ridley sea turtle (left)

less than 100 pounds (45 kg). The carapace is 23 to 27 inches (58 to 68 centimeters) long.

The other types of sea turtles range in weight from 100 to 450 pounds (45 to 203 kg).

17

On Land and Sea

A sea turtle's legs are paddle-shaped, like flippers. To swim, sea turtles move both of their front flippers forward at the same time—like a bird flapping its wings. They use their hind flippers as rudders. Sea turtles are among the fastest swimmers of all four-footed animals.

Sea turtles have strong, paddle-shaped flippers (left). A sea turtle uses its powerful front flippers to move forward in the water (below).

It takes a lot of effort for a sea turtle to move on land (above). Tracks left on the sand by a sea turtle (right)

On land, however, sea turtles are clumsy and slow. When females come ashore to lay their eggs, they pull themselves along by using their front flippers one after the other. They drag their bodies along the ground, leaving huge tracks in the sand.

Female sea turtles use a lot of energy coming ashore, digging a nest, and laying their eggs. They are exhausted after the effort. On shore, they cannot back up if something is in their way. They must circle around it.

Eyes, Ears, Mouth, and Nose

Sea turtles have no teeth. A sea turtle uses its sharp beak to cut its food.

Leatherbacks are not equipped with strong jaws. They feed on jellyfish. Hawksbills feed along coral reefs on sponges, shellfish, jellyfish, and seaweed.

A sea turtle's mouth is like a sharp beak (above). A loggerhead sea turtle feeding on a lobster (left)

Loggerheads use their power-ful jaws to eat shellfish, as well as fish, sponges, and jellyfish. Green turtles and ridleys feed mainly on seaweed.

A sea turtle's eyes are adapted for underwater vision.

Sea turtles' eyes are adapted to underwater vision. They are short-sighted on land. At night, however, sea turtles can see better on land than humans can. This is important, since nighttime is when the female sea turtles come ashore to lay eggs.

Turtle Tears?

Some people think sea turtles cry. Actually, the turtles are just excreting salt. Sea turtles take in large amounts of salt from the water and from their food. The excess salt is excreted from glands near their tear ducts.

Sea turtles have no external ears. Their eardrums are covered with skin. They hear low notes best, and are sensitive to vibrations on land and in the water.

Sea turtles can hold their breath for a long time underwater. When they come to the water's surface to breathe, they can take in great amounts of air. Under the water, their lungs extract every bit of oxygen.

Sea turtles can stay
underwater for a long time.

A hawksbill sea turtle resting under a reef of coral

When a sea turtle sinks to the bottom of the ocean to sleep, its body temperature drops. If the turtle is near a shore, it may sleep under a rocky ledge below the surface. Sea turtles use less oxygen in colder water.

Mating and Nesting

Most of our information about sea turtles comes from studying their nesting habits, eggs, and hatchlings.

Sea turtles mate near the shore. The male uses his sharp claw on each front flipper to hold the female. Sea turtles do not mate every year.

Six species of sea turtles dig their nests along the North, Central, and South American coasts and on some Caribbean islands. Popular nesting sites are along the coasts of Florida, the Gulf of Mexico in the United States, and the east and west coasts of Costa Rica.

Females often return to the place they were born to lay their eggs. Some swim thousands of miles to return to a certain beach.

Each female comes ashore several times in spring and early summer to nest. First, the female selects a spot on the beach

Most sea turtles wait until night-time to come ashore and lay their eggs.

A sea turtle digs a large hole in the sand (left) before laying her eggs (right).

above the high-water mark at high tide. This will keep the eggs from being washed away. The eggs will not hatch if they are soaked in water.

The female uses her front flippers to dig a large hole in the sand. Into this hole, the female lays between 50 and 150 eggs.

After she lays her eggs, a sea turtle covers the nest with sand (left) and then returns to the ocean (right).

The eggs look like large ping-pong balls.

After the female lays her eggs, she covers the nest with sand and returns to the sea. The sand keeps the eggs at the right temperature during incubation. The sun's heat helps the eggs hatch in about six weeks.

Hatchlings

A hatchling pecks its way out of its shell by using a sharp tooth on its beak. This is called an egg tooth. The hatchlings may take more than a day to come out of their shells. Each hatchling is only about 2 inches (5 centimeters) long.

All of the hatchlings must wiggle and dig their way up through

This baby sea turtle has just hatched from its shell (top left). Newly hatched sea turtles dig their way up through the sand (bottom left), and then find their way to the sea (above).

the sand at the same time. One hatchling could not do this alone.

All the species except the Kemp's ridley emerge at night. The hatchlings find their way to the sea by light reflected off the ocean.

Predators

Many predators hunt for turtle eggs. Coyotes, raccoons, foxes, feral pigs, and birds like to eat the eggs.

And when they hatch, the tiny hatchlings may be killed by predators before they even get to the sea. Only about ten per-cent will make it to the ocean.

A mammal called the coati (above) is one of many animals that prey on sea turtle eggs or hatchlings. Once in the sea, the hatchlings are in danger of being caught by crabs or other sea animals (left).

Of those that reach the ocean, many will be caught by crabs, sharks, and other large fish.

Humans, however, are the greatest predators of sea turtles and sea-turtle eggs.

Adult turtles are caught by people who enjoy turtle meat or turtle soup. Many countries list sea turtles as endangered species, and forbid catching and killing them. But some people break the laws.

Many conservationists dig up newly laid turtle eggs and take them to a protected beach. Some nesting sites are protected in state or national parks. Also,

In some places, conservationists dig up sea-turtle eggs (above) and bring them to a beach where they will be protected. At sea turtle farms (right), the turtles are raised in a protected environment. Later, they are released into the wild.

turtle farms have been established, including a large turtle farm on Grand Cayman Island.

"TEDS"

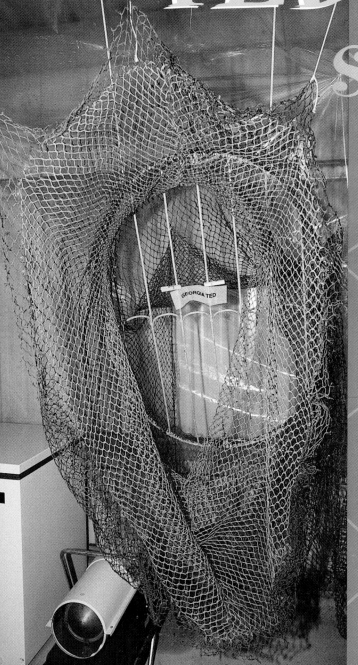

Sea turtles are often caught in nets used by people who fish for shrimp. The turtles drown when caught in shrimpers' nets because they cannot surface to breathe. Now, many states require shrimpers to use turtle-excluding devices, or TEDs.

The Future

Sea turtles have other problems, too. In some areas, hotels and apartment buildings now line the shores where turtles once laid their eggs.

Automobile headlights and lights from nearby buildings may frighten female sea turtles, and the sudden bright light of a flash camera sends the turtles

ATTENTION BEACH USERS
- HELP PROTECT ENDANGERED SEA TURTLES
- AVOID DISTURBING NESTING FEMALES
- LEAVE NEST, EGGS AND HATCHLINGS UNDISTURBED
- TURN OFF LIGHTS THAT SHINE ON BEACH
  (BETWEEN MAY 1ST - OCT. 31ST)
SEA TURTLES ARE PROTECTED BY COUNTY STATE AND FEDERAL LAW. FINES UP TO $20,000.
FOR MORE INFO, CONTACT 63_-2016

At some nesting sites, signs ask people not to disturb the sea turtles.

scurrying back to the sea. Each year, there are fewer and fewer beaches where sea turtles feel safe enough to come ashore and nest.

But many people want to see these ancient creatures survive.

And they are trying to make sure that the sea turtles get all the protection and help they need.

A female sea turtle makes her way back to the sea.

To Find Out More

Here are some additional resources to help you learn more about sea turtles.

 **Books**

 **Online Sites**

Ancona, George, **Turtle Watch.** Macmillan Publishing Co., 1987.

Gibbons, Gail, **Sea Turtles.** Holiday House, 1995.

Serventy, Vincent, **Turtle and Tortoise.** Raintree Childrens Books, 1985.

Switzer, Merebeth, **Nature's Children: Turtles**. Grolier, 1986.

International Marine Mammal Project
http://www.marinemammal @igc.apc.org

Sea Turtle Restoration Project
http://www.seaturtles@igc. apc.org

Earth Island
http://www.earthisland.org/ ei/strp/strpca.html

Turtle Trax—A Marine Turtle Page
http://www.io.org/~bunrab/

Organizations

Archie Carr Center for Sea Turtle Research
Bartram Hall
University of Florida
Gainesville, Florida 32611
904-392-5194
904-392-9166 (fax)

Conservation International
The Marine Turtle Newsletter
1015 Eighteenth Street, NW
Suite 1000
Washington, DC 20036

Earth Island Institute
300 Broadway, Suite 28
San Francisco, CA 94133-3312

Center for Marine Conservation
1725 DeSales Street, NW,
Suite 500
Washington, DC 20036

Washington Wildlife Alliance
2319 N. 45th Street, #203
Seattle, WA 98103
206-633-3435
206-633-3488 (fax)

Important Words

adapt to adjust to new conditions

conservationist a person whose job it is to protect and preserve wildlife

dominate to rule over

emerge to come out

endangered a species that is in danger of extinction

excrete to throw off or eliminate from the body

external on the outside

extinction the destruction or wiping out of something

incubation the time during which an egg develops while getting ready to hatch

predator an animal that lives by killing and eating other animals

streamlined sleek, designed to move quickly through air or water

Index

Meet the Author

Emilie U. Lepthien received her B.A. and M.S. degrees and certificate in school administration from Northwestern University. She taught upper-grade science and social studies, and was a school principal in Chicago, Illinois, for twenty years. For Children's Press, she has written books in the *Enchantment of the World, True Book,* and *America the Beautiful* series.